SEATTLE

A PHOTOGRAPHIC PORTRAIT II

Photography by Stuart Westmorland
Narrative by Barbara Sleeper

TWIN LIGHTS PUBLISHERS | ROCKPORT, MASSACHUSETTS

First published in the United States of America by:

Twin Lights Publishers, Inc.
51 Broadway
Rockport, Massachusetts 01966
Telephone: (978) 546-7398
http://www.twinlightspub.com

ISBN: 978-1-934907-16-0

10 9 8 7 6 5 4 3 2

(*opposite*)
Experience Music Project Museum
and Seattle Space Needle

(*frontispiece*)
Seattle Public Market

(*jacket front*)
Seattle Space Needle

Book design by:
SYP Design & Production, Inc.
www.sypdesign.com

Printed in China

Introduction

Mention the name Seattle and an affectionate list of descriptives come to mind: evergreen trees, double rainbows, rugged mountains, sparkling water, tech geeks and totem poles, boats galore, volcanoes, salmon, rain – beautiful! You'd also have to add the words artistic, entrepreneurial, and free-spirited to capture the true essence of this Pacific Northwest gem.

Seattle has a fascinating and often humorous history. The first white settlers arrived in 1851 and established their fledgling town called Duwamps on the mudflats of Elliott Bay. The bustling lumber town was soon renamed Seattle in honor of Chief Sealth, the kind and insightful leader of the Duwamish, Suquamish, and Allied tribes of Puget Sound, who first befriended and helped the struggling early settlers. By the time the Territorial Legislature incorporated the City of Seattle in 1869, the population had swelled to more than 2,000 residents.

Then overnight, the Klondike Gold Rush of 1897-1898 turned Seattle into an instant boomtown outfitting thousands of hopeful prospectors heading north. Rapid growth followed and Seattle quickly evolved into a popular trade and shipping center with Asia and the North Pacific. To celebrate all of this success, Seattle hosted the 1909 Alaska-Yukon-Pacific Exposition attended by more than 3.5 million people. Seattle did it again in 1962 when it hosted the futuristic Century 21 Exposition or Seattle World's Fair, attended by nearly 10 million people.

Today, Seattle is a prosperous metropolis of 3.5 million people, loaded with culture and art, tall skyscrapers, award-winning restaurants, and the non-stop action of four pro sports teams. Walk the streets and you can see and feel the can-do energy: Seattle is famous for its spirit of optimism and enterprise. This "Seattle Spirit" made it possible to connect Lake Washington and Puget Sound via a ship canal and locks, build the world's largest man-made island at the mouth of the Duwamish River, and construct the $1.96 billion SR 99 Tunnel Project for two miles beneath Seattle.

Yes, Seattleites are a wild bunch. We buy more sunglasses, boats and coffee, read more books, see more movies and are more college-educated than most folks. We also have the most glass-blowing studios outside of Murano, Italy. In 1996 we were voted "the most honest city" and in 2005 "the most fit." Not surprising, it was here that the Smiley Face originated, along with the Wave, and we are still trying to make "Louie Louie" our State Song.

In short, Seattle is a joyful, playful city whose exuberant energy is beautifully captured in Stuart Westmorland's photography. It's a great place to enjoy the outdoors, hug a dog, raise your kids, smell the marine air, enjoy a romantic sunset – or just kick back and savor the "boogie woogie" of our magical city.

Welcome to "Wild Salmon Country!"

Pike Place Seafood Market

Seattle is famous for fresh seafood and there is no better place to buy it than at the historic Pike Place Market. Here a vendor holds two cooked Dungeness crabs ready to grab and go. Victor Steinbrueck Park at the north end of the market is a great place to enjoy a crab picnic on a sunny day.

Kerry Park *(top)*

A rare Super Moon rises from the East as the Seattle Space Needle and modern city buildings light up for the night. This beautiful view of the Emerald City is the reason residents, tourists and photographers alike, flock to Kerry Park located on Queen Anne Hill just north of downtown.

Seattle Waterfront *(bottom)*

A freighter cruises slowly past the Seattle skyline at dusk. Framed by the Space Needle to the left and the now tiny historic Smith Tower to the right, this peaceful scene was captured from Hamilton Viewpoint Park in West Seattle. The red flowering currant blooming in the foreground is a popular native plant.

Seattle Space Needle *(opposite)*

Built for the Seattle World's Fair in 1962, the Space Needle celebrated its 50th birthday in 2012. Now the iconic symbol of Seattle recognized around the world, the 605-foot-high flying saucer on hourglass legs was returned to its original color, retro "Galaxy gold," for the year-long festivities.

Seattle Viewpoint

Pink cosmos brighten a popular image of downtown Seattle taken from Kerry Park. Mt. Rainier, an active volcano located 54 miles southeast of the city, is always a visual treat on a sunny day. This snow-capped landmark rises 14,411 feet above sea level, making it tall enough to generate its own weather patterns.

Westlake Park

Numerous park benches, a walk-through waterfall, artfully engraved pavers, and humorous sculptures of metal figures, many wearing knit scarves, make this a restful place to take a break in downtown Seattle. Artist Konstantin Dimopoulos painted 16 tree trunks bright ultramarine blue as part of the "Blue Tree Project" to protest global deforestation.

Century Square Clock

Old-fashioned street lights and an antique clock enhance the charm of Westlake Park. The park is considered Seattle's "town square," used for public events and the annual Holiday Carousel. Nearby, at the Westlake Center transportation hub, you can catch the Seattle Center Monorail, South Lake Union Streetcar, Metro buses, or Sound Transit's Link Light Rail.

Fremont Rocket

This WWII Fairchild C-119 tail boom, modified to look like a rocket then attached to the side of a building, is typical of the wild and wacky artwork found throughout Seattle's Fremont area. Since the 1970s, many Fremont residents have declared their eclectic neighborhood "The Center of the Universe."

Fremont Troll

Children love to climb on this engaging sculpture hidden beneath the north end of the Aurora Bridge in Seattle's freaky Fremont district. Created in 1990, the 18-foot-tall cement troll, crushing a Volkswagen Beetle in its left hand, best epitomizes Fremont's spirited motto: *"De Libertas Quirkas,"* meaning Freedom to be Peculiar.

Northwest Folklife Festival *(top)*

Thousands gather around the *International Fountain* at Seattle Center to celebrate the annual Folklife Festival. Held over Memorial Day Weekend, the festival showcases the evolving traditions of the Pacific Northwest. It is just one of 5,000 events held at the Seattle Center each year that attracts more than 12 million visitors.

Log House Museum *(bottom)*

This restored 1904 building houses the "Birthplace of Seattle" Log House Museum. Sponsored by the Southwest Seattle Historical Society, the museum celebrates the fascinating history of the Duwamish Peninsula and the first settlers that landed here in 1851, which included 10 adults and 12 children aboard the schooner *Exact*.

Seattle Center

Kids enjoy summer fun at the *International Fountain*. Designed as a modernist water sculpture for the 1962 Seattle World's Fair, it has more than 20 spigots that shoot water out in computer-controlled patterns. The 74-acre Seattle Center campus is home to more than 30 cultural, educational, sports, and entertainment organizations.

Rainbow Valley Mural (top)

Painted in 1998 by Carlos Callejo, Deborah Bigelow and Joan Robbins on the Darigold building in Rainier Valley, the mural playfully captures Seattle's melting pot history. Featured in five panels is Jimi Hendrix along with people from every ethnic background. Chief Seattle presides over the acrylic crowd with outstretched arms.

Nordic Heritage Mural (bottom)

Bergen Place, located in the heart of Ballard's business district, is named after Bergen, Norway, one of Seattle's International Sister Cities. In 1995, Canadian artists Mike Svob and Alan Wylie painted this intricate mural depicting Ballard's rich Norwegian heritage. The following year, it was dedicated by the King and Queen of Norway.

Friends of Post Alley Mural *(top)*

Renowned Seattle artist Billy King painted this colorful, much-photographed mural in 2002 on a sliding WWII metal blackout door. Measuring 9 x 25 feet, the mural is visibly prominent, mounted on a brick wall at the intersection of Second Avenue and Yesler Way in the Pioneer Square Historic District.

Underwater Dreamscape Mural *(bottom)*

This larger-than-life mural covers an entire building in Pioneer Square. Painted by renowned contemporary artist Jeff "Weirdo" Jacobson in 2010, it reflects his skillful juxtaposition of hyper-realistic images with otherworldly creations. "I've finally reached a point where there's no filter between my imagination and the canvas," says Jacobson.

Olympic Iliad *(opposite)*

The 60x30-foot steel sculpture by Alexander Liberman was installed near the Space Needle in 1984. The Glass House (left), is part of the exquisite Chihuly Garden and Glass exhibit opened in 2012. The EMP Museum also opened the Icons of Science Fiction Exhibit in 2012 to help celebrate the 50th Anniversary of the 1962 Seattle World's Fair.

Typewriter Eraser, Scale X *(above)*

Claes Olenburg and Coosje van Brugeen created this by-gone office relic as part of an artists' series transforming mundane objects into a massive scale. On display at the Olympic Sculpture Park, the whimsical piece, was loaned to the Seattle Art Museum by Microsoft co-founder Paul Allen, who has done much to energize Seattle.

New Archetypes *(opposite)*

These towering and toppled stainless steel sculptures were created in 1990 by Anne and Patrick Poirier. The shiny metal artwork is positioned for maximum effect throughout the courtyard next to the Washington Mutual Bank Building on Second Avenue. This is another wonderful example of Seattle's abundant public art.

Icon Grill *(top)*

Famous for its "aroused" Americana cooking that features comfort staples such as macaroni and cheese, fried chicken and meatloaf, the Icon Grill is as much a taste bud pleaser as it is an art lover's paradise. The restaurant showcases the blown glass artwork of Martin Blank as well as the work of many other local artists.

David Huchthausen's Loft *(bottom)*

David Huchthausen has played a vital role in the evolution of glass into a fine art form. His intricate sculptures are included in 65 major museums and hundreds of exhibitions worldwide. Huchthausen creates his enigmatic artwork in his Seattle studio, capturing the magical interplay of refracted light and shadow in each piece.

Great Wheel (opposite)

Aglow at sunset, the Great Wheel is one of the newest attractions along Seattle's bustling waterfront. Located at the end of Pier 57, the giant Ferris wheel is lit up each night with white gondola lights. During holidays and home games for the Seahawks, Sounders and Mariners, the wheel pulsates with colorful LED lightshows.

Seattlescape (top)

This golden panoramic view of downtown Seattle was taken from Beacon Hill at sunset. Like Rome, the Emerald City is built on seven hills. Bisected by the pulsing north-south artery of Interstate 5, and dominated by the 76-story Columbia Center, Seattle is a cosmopolitan city that still retains its small town feel.

Georgetown Hat n' Boots (bottom)

The colossal, 44-foot-wide hat and 22-foot-tall cowboy boots were designed by Seattle artist Lewis Nasmyth in 1953. Installed at the "Premium Tex" gas station, the kitschy road art attracted a stampede of customers. Considered the "soul of Georgetown," these treasures are now permanently preserved in Oxbow Park.

Father and Son (above)

Created in 2005 by artist Louise Bour-geois for Seattle's Olympic Sculpture Park, this sentimental fountain features a father and young son reaching out to each other. Only one figure is visible at a time, the other covered by cascading water. Once an hour a bell rings and the water level changes to reveal the other figure.

Olympic Sculpture Park (opposite)

Called *The Eagle*, this giant, bright red stainless steel sculpture was created by Alexander Calder in 1971. Gifted to the Seattle Art Museum by Mary and Jon Shirley, the 39-foot-tall metal bird is now perched in the Olympic Sculpture Park, a nine-acre industrial site transformed into a stunning green space for public art.

Lightning over Seattle (pages 26 – 27)

This is the electrifying image that first launched Stuart Westmorland's photography career. The photo dramatically illustrates why the Space Needle has 25 lightning rods on its roof to prevent damage from such wild storms. Luckily, electrical disturbances like this are rare due to Seattle's relatively mild climate.

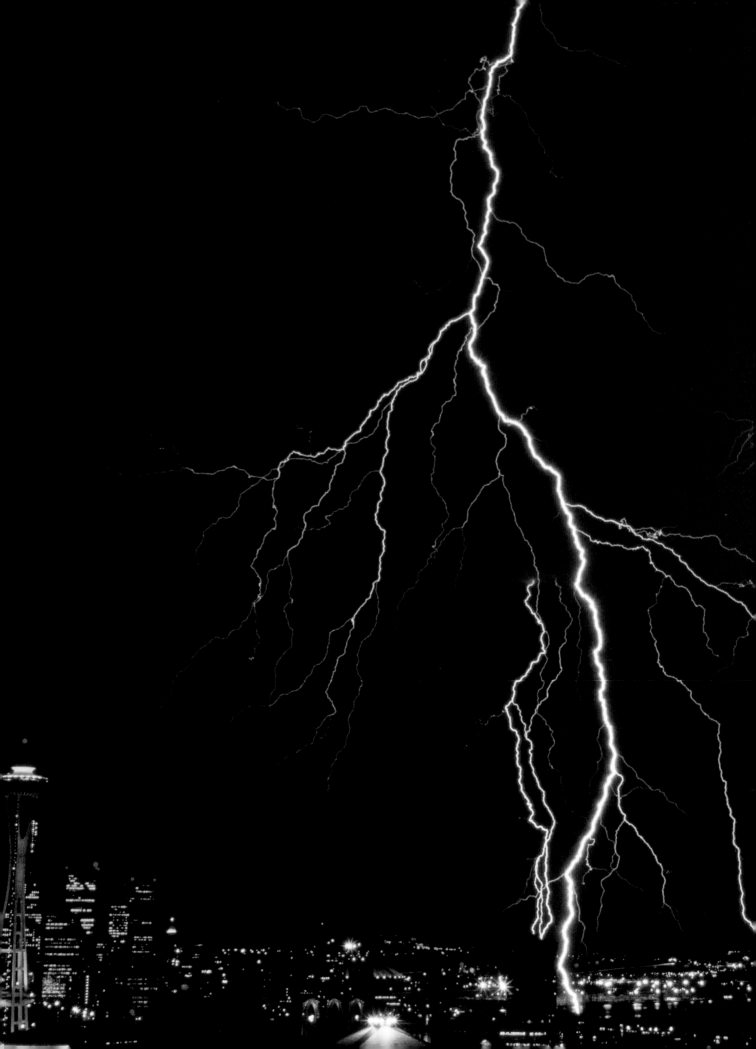

Seattle Central Library (opposite, top)

The Seattle public library system was established in 1890 and includes the Central Library and 26 branches. Encompassing eleven levels and 362,987 square feet, the library has free WiFi access, 400 computers, and over 1 million items in its collection. Underground parking makes this avant-garde educational center easily accessible.

Library Architecture (opposite, bottom)

Renowned Dutch architect Rem Koolhaas wrapped this award-winning library in a paned-glass skin. Flooded with natural light, the library opened in 2004. Visitors are encouraged to take self-guided tours to explore the stimulating color, art, and sculptures on every floor. Don't miss the 10th-floor atrium for a breathtaking view.

Sea-Tac International Airport (above)

In a celebration of technology, aviation, and glass, Fentress Bradburn Architects of Denver designed this spectacular 60-by-350-foot glass wall in the Central Terminal of the Seattle-Tacoma airport. This "portal to space warp" overlooks busy runways and the Olympic Mountains. It can also flex up to eleven inches during an earthquake.

Belltown P-Patch Community Gardens

It took six years and thousands of volunteer hours to transform this once vacant city lot into a lovely open space and community garden in downtown Seattle. The Belltown P-Patch is a working park that contains 40 garden "patches" for use by neighborhood residents. Take a stroll here and feel the community spirit.

DO NOT BE AFRAID
OF OVERFEEDING
SEAGULLS ARE
DAINTY EATERS.

Ivar's Seagulls

As a squawking tribute to their famous mentor, Ivar Haglund, seagulls perform aerial maneuvers for French fries at Ivar's Acres of Clams. People have been encouraged to "feed the gulls" since 1938 when Ivar first opened his "keep clam" seafood eatery at Pier 54. The skilled moochers catch food in mid-air or take it "gently" from your fingers.

Great Wheel

Attached to the end of Miners Landing on Pier 57, the 17-story Great Wheel is framed to the left by the Seattle Aquarium and to the right by Seattle's major sports venues, Century Link Field and Safeco Field. On Seahawks, Sounders, or Mariners game days, boisterous sports fans spill out of the stadiums throughout downtown Seattle.

The Seattle Aquarium *(top)*

Located at Pier 59, The Seattle Aquarium attracts more than 800,000 visitors each year. It is home to playful sea otters, aquabatic harbor seals, undulating jellyfish, and colorful fish of every kind. Catch a glimpse of Puget Sound's sixgill shark, the third-largest predatory shark in the world, or the giant Pacific octopus that can weigh up to 100 pounds.

Wolf-Eel *(bottom)*

More than 40,000 school children visit the Seattle Aquarium each year. Here kids get a close look at one of Puget Sound's most intriguing residents, a wolf-eel, which is native to the northern Pacific Ocean. Weighing up to 40 pounds and reaching lengths over six feet, these eel-like fish crush their crustacean food with their strong jaws.

Myrtle Edwards Park *(above)*

The Seattle Art Museum enhanced the Elliott Bay shoreline by creating this "pocket beach" within Myrtle Edwards Park. The park offers 1.25 miles of winding bike and pedestrian paths along Elliott Bay, picnic tables, a fishing pier, and awesome views of brilliant sunsets behind the Olympic Mountains.

West Point Lighthouse *(opposite, top)*

Discovery Park is Seattle's largest public park with 534 acres of meadows, forests, and beaches and nearly 12 miles of hiking trails. It is an excellent place to view wildlife, especially marine mammals and birds. The park's historic West Point Lighthouse, opened in 1881, is on the National Register of Historic Places.

Alki Point Lighthouse *(opposite, bottom)*

Located at the southern entrance to Elliott Bay, this picturesque lighthouse began as a coal-fed lens-lantern atop a post in 1887. Now, crowded by a backdrop of homes in West Seattle, the Alki Point Lighthouse is one of 13 working lighthouses positioned around Puget Sound. On foggy days, ferries blow their horns every two minutes.

Aquatic Tailgate Party

Boaters with "Husky Fever" anchor their yachts in Union Bay then shuttle by water taxi to the University of Washington Husky Football Stadium for home games. This scenic view of Lake Washington, the SR-520 floating bridge, and Bellevue skyscrapers can be seen from the stadium.

Statue of Liberty Plaza

Celebrating the 40th anniversary of the Boy Scouts of America, this *Little Sisters of Liberty* statue was presented by the BSA to the City of Seattle in 1952. More than 200 1/8-size replicas of the Statue of Liberty were placed in 39 states and four American Territories as "a reminder of the value of liberty and freedom cherished by all."

Wingtip View of Seattle *(opposite, top)*

Olde Thyme Aviation, located at the Museum of Flight at Boeing Field, offers aerial tours of Seattle in authentically restored antique airplanes. Here passengers dressed in old-time barnstorming regalia get a bird's-eye-view of Seattle, Lake Union, and Gasworks Park in a WWII Waco UPF-7 biplane.

Lake Union Houseboats *(opposite, bottom)*

The best way to view one of Seattle's most charming waterfront lifestyles is by kayak. Seattle's picturesque houseboat community – the largest east of the Orient – encircles part of Lake Union, Portage Bay, and the Ship Canal. Tour guides are quick to point out the famous houseboat featured in the movie *Sleepless in Seattle*.

Shilshole Bay Marina *(above)*

Sailboats race past the Port of Seattle's Shilshole Bay Marina located in Ballard. With more than 1,400 slips filled with yachts of every size and description, the marina is the perfect place to learn how to sail or begin a boating adventure on Puget Sound – Washington's 100-mile-long inland sea.

Ride the Ducks *(top)*

Tourists ride in an amphibious WWII vehicle through "funky" Fremont. Piloted by a Coast Guard-certified "crazy captain" who sings and quacks jokes, the 90-minute tour includes a narrated dip in Lake Union plus a land cruise past popular city sights. It's the best way to see Seattleites dancing to live music on the sidewalks of Pioneer Square.

Fishermen's Terminal *(bottom)*

Located on Salmon Bay in the Interbay neighborhood, Fishermen's Terminal serves more than 600 vessels, including several featured on Discovery Channel's *Deadliest Catch*. Every September, the Fall Fishermen's Festival celebrates the return of the North Pacific Fishing Fleet to the terminal, where it has been based for nearly a century.

Seattle Fishermen's Memorial *(opposite)*

The Fishermen's Memorial is a bronze and stone sculpture with plaques memorializing more than 675 local commercial fishermen and women who have lost their lives at sea since the beginning of the 20th century. It is a somber reminder of how dangerous the North Pacific fishing industry can be.

Seattle Skyline

Seattle is a water city with an endless variety of waterfront lifestyles and scenic views. Connected to the Pacific Ocean via Puget Sound, the busy Port of Seattle hosts everything from cruise ships, freighters, ferries, and Navy vessels to the gas turbine *Victoria Clipper IV* that travels to Victoria, BC at speeds of 50 miles per hour.

Boating Season Opens *(opposite)*

Decorated with festive flags, vessels line up in Portage Bay for the Opening Day Boat Parade through Montlake Cut. Sponsored by the Seattle Yacht Club, this annual celebration takes place the first Saturday in May to kick off the summer boating season.

Steaming Through *(top)*

The historic Montlake drawbridge opens for the boat parade. Letting off steam, the *Virginia V* is the last operating Puget Sound "Mosquito Fleet" steamer. She was once part of a large fleet of small passenger and freight-carrying ships that linked the islands and ports of Puget Sound in the late 19th and early 20th centuries.

Boat Parade *(bottom)*

The *Honey Bee* (left) and another parade boat cruise past the Laurelhurst neighborhood on Union Bay, the birthplace of Bill Gates. Just a week after the Opening Day festivities end, more than 30 tugboats will gather in Elliott Bay for the annual Seattle Tugboat Race Championships, the largest tugboat race in the world.

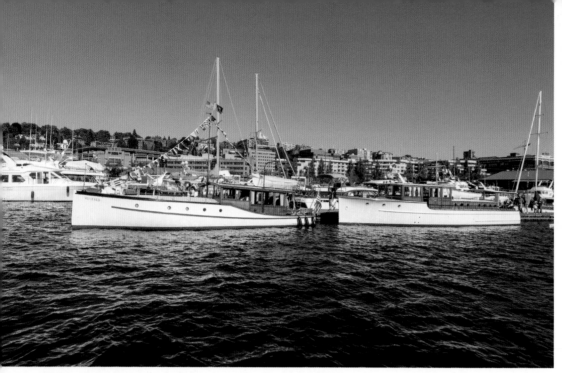

Wooden Boat Festival (top)

Every June, The Center for Wooden Boats hosts the annual Wooden Boat Festival at South Lake Union. It's the best time to see classic wooden boats like the *Winifred* (left), build your own tiny wooden ship, go for a free ride on a historic CWB boat, or rent a miniature sailboat to glide across the Model Boat Pond at Lake Union Park.

The Center for Wooden Boats (bottom)

Seattle has more pleasure boats per capita than anywhere else in the U.S. The Center for Wooden Boats is a hands-on, living museum that celebrates our rich and varied small craft heritage by preserving and sharing both the boats and the time-tested maritime skills of sailing, paddling, boatbuilding, and boat maintenance.

Native American Totem Poles

Ancestral Native Americans carved totem poles using beaver teeth and clamshells. Modern carvers now use crook knives and adzes. The Honor Pole raised at The Center for Wooden Boats was a gift from the Tlingit people of Alaska. At the top are carved an Eagle and a Raven, the two principle crests of the Tlingit Nation.

Seattle Skyline *(pages 48 – 49)*

Cast in warm sunset hues, the Seattle skyline is mesmerizing from Seacrest Park in West Seattle. Seacrest Park is a superb destination for a romantic date, for scuba diving in the park's three shoreline coves, or to catch a 10-minute ride on the King County Water Taxi to downtown Seattle.

Summer Sunset *(above)*

The flaming red sun sets behind the silhouetted Olympic Mountains on a beautiful summer evening at Ballard's Golden Gardens Park. Seattleites know how to maximize outdoor fun during the dry season from July through September with almost a manic energy, because all too soon the rains will return once again.

Golden Gardens Park

Seattle has 400 parks and open areas encompassing over 6,200 acres of parkland. Here residents enjoy a beach walk and rock skipping at Golden Gardens Park north of Shilshole Bay Marina. Sheltered from severe weather by Puget Sound, the park is popular for kitesurfing, sailboarding, and other wind-driven sports.

Washington State Ferries

Two ferries depart the Seattle Waterfront, one heading across Elliott Bay to Bremerton and the other to Bainbridge Island. Washington State Ferries (WSF) is the largest ferry system in the United States with 10 routes and 20 terminals served by 22 vessels. WSF carries 10 million vehicles and more than 22 million people each year.

Mt. Rainier

This dramatic photograph of Mt. Rainier towering 14,411 feet over Puget Sound was taken onboard a Washington State ferry at the Kingston terminal on Whidbey Island. John Muir climbed Mt. Rainier in 1888 and it became a national park in 1899. It is the highest and most potentially dangerous active volcano in the Cascade Range.

Harbor Seal

California sea lions snoozing on buoy platforms and harbor seals resting along the shores of Puget Sound are a common sight. Newborn harbor seal pups need to rest and regulate their body temperature while their mothers feed. This pup will turn a spotted silver-gray to brown or black as an adult, and reach a length of up to six feet.

Breaching Orca

An important animal totem to Native Americans in the Pacific Northwest, a mighty orca, or "sea wolf," breaches in Puget Sound. Pods of orcas, designated J, K and L, are frequently spotted in the waters around San Juan Island, but they can also be seen in Puget Sound. Whale watching trips are available from Seattle to the San Juan Islands.

Space Needle Observation Deck *(above)*

Visitors enjoy a 360° view of Seattle after a scenic elevator ride to 520 feet. The panoramic view of Puget Sound, Mt. Rainier, the Olympic and Cascade mountain ranges, and seaplanes buzzing Lake Union is breathtaking. Guests can use complimentary Swarovski telescopes to spy on cruise ships departing Bell Street Pier for Alaska.

May Peace Prevail *(opposite)*

Equivalent to a 60-story building, the 9,550-ton Space Needle with rotating Sky-City restaurant rises 605 feet at its highest point. At its steel feet rests an even more powerful symbol: May Peace Prevail on Earth. In 2001, the United Nations General Assembly declared the 21st of September the International Day of Peace.

Pacific Science Center (above)

A stegosaurus wades past the iconic, cathedral-like Gothic arches at Seattle's famous science museum. At night the white arches are lit in dramatic colors to match current civic events. The 8-building complex was designed in 1962 by Minoru Yamasaki who also designed the twin towers of New York 's World Trade Center.

Seattle Center Monorail (opposite, top)

Resembling a "smashed guitar," the colorful metal exterior of the EMP Museum is a monumental sculpture unto itself. The museum celebrates popular music, science fiction, and pop culture. Departing every 10 minutes, the Seattle Center Monorail runs through part of the EMP building as it heads downtown to Westlake Center.

Tyrannosaurus Rex (opposite, bottom)

This toothy carnivore greets visitors at the Pacific Science Center. Along with a permanent dinosaur display, this fun learning center, includes two IMAX theaters, one of the world's largest Laser Dome theaters, a tropical butterfly house, tide pool, planetarium, and hundreds of hands-on science exhibits.

Seattle George Monument (above)

Installed near the Washington State Convention and Trade Center in 1989, this unique sculpture by Buster Simpson simultaneously portrays Chief Seattle and George Washington. A tripod supports a torso planter and the monument's head – Washington's profile as a weather vane encircling twenty-four aluminum profiles of Chief Seattle fanned out to create an armature for English ivy growing out of a Boeing 707 nose cone.

Freeway Park (left)

The idea for a downtown city park to conceal part of Interstate 5 took shape in 1966. Ten years later, the 5.2-acre park became a reality – beautifully landscaped with sculptures, a decorative fountain, and lush vegetation. Freeway Park is located next to the Washington State Convention and Trade Center.

Historic Smith Tower View *(above)*

When completed in 1914, the 42-story Smith Tower was the tallest building in Seattle and the fourth tallest building in the world. It remained Seattle's tallest building until 1962 when the Space Needle was built. The Observation Deck on the 35th floor offers a bird's-eye-view of downtown Seattle, cruise ships in port, and a dwarfed Space Needle in the distance.

Wishing Chair *(right)*

The Smith Tower's Chinese Room was furnished by the last Empress of China and features a hand-carved wood and porcelain-inlay ceiling, ornately-carved Blackwood furniture and 17th-century work panels. Legend holds that single women who sit in the Wishing Chair will be married within a year.

William Henry Seward Statue

The life-size bronze statue of America's famous statesman stands in front of the Volunteer Park Conservatory. Sculpted by Richard E. Brooks, it was unveiled in 1909 at the Alaska-Yukon-Pacific Exposition and later moved here. Seward was best known for his successful brokerage of the purchase of Alaska from Russia in 1867.

Volunteer Park Conservatory

Modeled after London's Crystal Palace, this stately Victorian-style greenhouse was built in 1912 using 3,426 panes of glass carefully fitted into an ornate wood and iron frame-work. The conservatory features tropical plants, a fascinating cactus collection, seasonal floral displays, and exquisite blooming orchids, all from around the world.

Autumn in the Garden *(top)*

The blazing colors of autumn are best enjoyed during a tranquil stroll through the Seattle Japanese Garden located in the Washington Park Arboretum. This beautiful 3.5-acre sanctuary, accented with Asian sculptures and landscaping, was planned by world-renowned garden designer Juki Iida. It is at peak bloom during mid-May.

Japanese Garden *(bottom)*

Content turtles and goldfish inhabit the peaceful lily-pad pond at Seattle's Japanese Garden. Seasonal activities include an annual display of local bonsai collections, the celebration of the Japanese Star Festival or Tanabata, moon viewing, and a day of cultural activities and performances each fall to honor the importance of elders.

Kubota Garden *(opposite)*

This artistically landscaped urban refuge honors the vision and lifework of Japanese emigrant Fujitaro Kubota. He started the now 20-acre garden in 1927 with the purchase of five acres of logged swampland in Seattle's Rainier Beach neighborhood. Kubota's dream was to display the beauty of the Northwest in a Japanese manner.

Carl S. English, Jr. Botanical Garden (top)

Newlyweds enjoy a quiet photo-op in the beautiful 7-acre Carl S. English, Jr. Botanical Garden. Named after the horticulturist who created them, the English-style gardens contain nearly 600 species and 1,500 varieties of plants from around the world, many gathered with the help of international ship captains passing through the Ballard Locks.

Garden Paradise (bottom)

The Pacific Northwest is a gardener's paradise. Plants love the mild climate and ample rainfall. Some species are so happy they bloom twice a year, in spring and fall. Unlike people, plants don't mind that Seattle gets the least amount of annual sunlight of all major cities in the lower-48 states.

Bellevue Botanical Garden

(opposite, top and bottom)

Rock towers defy gravity at this urban refuge that encompasses 53 acres of cultivated gardens, restored woodlands, and natural wetlands. The Garden d'Lights Festival held here each year features dazzling LED lights shaped into flowers, waterfalls, and glow-in-the-dark "critters."

Lincoln Park (above)

Located just north of the Fauntleroy Ferry Terminal in West Seattle, Lincoln Park offers residents 4.6 miles of walking trails, 3.9 miles of bike paths, acres of playfields, a mile of Puget Sound beaches to explore, picnic shelters, and an outdoor heated saltwater pool. This multi-purpose park is popular year-round.

Chief Seattle Gravesite (left)

Chief Seattle died on June 7, 1866 and is buried on the Port Madison Indian Reservation in Suquamish, WA. Every August, during Chief Seattle Days, a memorial tribute is held at his gravesite.

Grand Forest Park (opposite)

Hikers enjoy a stroll on the 3-mile trail system through Grand Forest Park on nearby Bainbridge Island.

Schmitz Preserve Park

A fallen tree has been converted into a toothy piece of art in West Seattle's 53-acre Schmitz Park. Located 15 blocks east of Alki Point, the preserve protects one of the last stands of undisturbed forest in Seattle. It is named after Ferdinand and Emma Schmitz who donated the first 30 acres to help create the park in 1908.

Quiet Retreat

Take a stroll on looping trails through the green-canopied oasis of Schmitz Preserve Park. Except for the paved entrance and a small corner parking lot, this peaceful city retreat has remained essentially unchanged. Some of the ancient cedar trees have been here long before the first white settlers arrived at Alki Point.

Snoqualmie Falls

A lone fisherman braves the damp mist created by the 268-foot Snoqualmie Falls. One hundred feet taller than Niagara Falls, this dramatic waterfall attracts more than 1.5 million visitors each year. The Salish Lodge and Spa, perched at the top of the falls, is a great place to spend a romantic day or weekend.

Waterfall Garden Park

This lovely little park near Pioneer Square recreates the soothing sound of a cascading mountain waterfall with 5,000 gallons of water per minute pouring over 22-foot-tall granite slabs. This dramatic gift was given to Seattle to honor the men and women of United Parcel Service, which began right here in 1907.

Woodland Park Zoo *(above)*

This comical meerkat posse is on high alert at Seattle's award-winning Woodland Park Zoo. The 92-acre wildlife oasis is home to over 300 different animal species. Considered one of the finest zoos in the world, WPZ is famous for its cutting-edge naturalistic exhibits and extensive horticultural collections visible throughout the zoo grounds.

Mountain Goats *(left)*

These sure-footed, high altitude climbers are native to Washington State. While it's possible to see the wooly-white bovines in the Cascade Mountains, the easiest place to spot one is at Seattle's Woodland Park Zoo. This Noah's Ark for animals successfully breeds many endangered species and works hard to save animals and habitats around the world.

Cougar Mountain Zoo

Located 15 miles East of Seattle in the town of Issaquah, the zoo sits on the north-facing slope of Cougar Mountain with commanding views of Lake Sammamish and the Cascade Mountains. Combining the beauty of wildlife with art, this unique zoo features the world's largest collection of bronze animal art and offers the popular holiday Reindeer Festival.

U.S. Navy Blue Angels *(top)*

The highlight of the Seattle Seafair Hydro-plane Races is the adrenalin-pumping Blue Angel's airshow performed right over the Lake Washington race course. Here the team illustrates their precision flying skills by performing close, breathtaking maneuvers in the six-jet Delta Formation.

Seattle Seafair *(bottom)*

The Blue Angels serve as positive role models and goodwill ambassadors for the U.S. Navy and Marine Corps. Seattle's I-90 Floating Bridge is closed during their performances as the jets circle, soar, dive, and roar all around the city. Seafair is definitely Seattle's crescendo summer party.

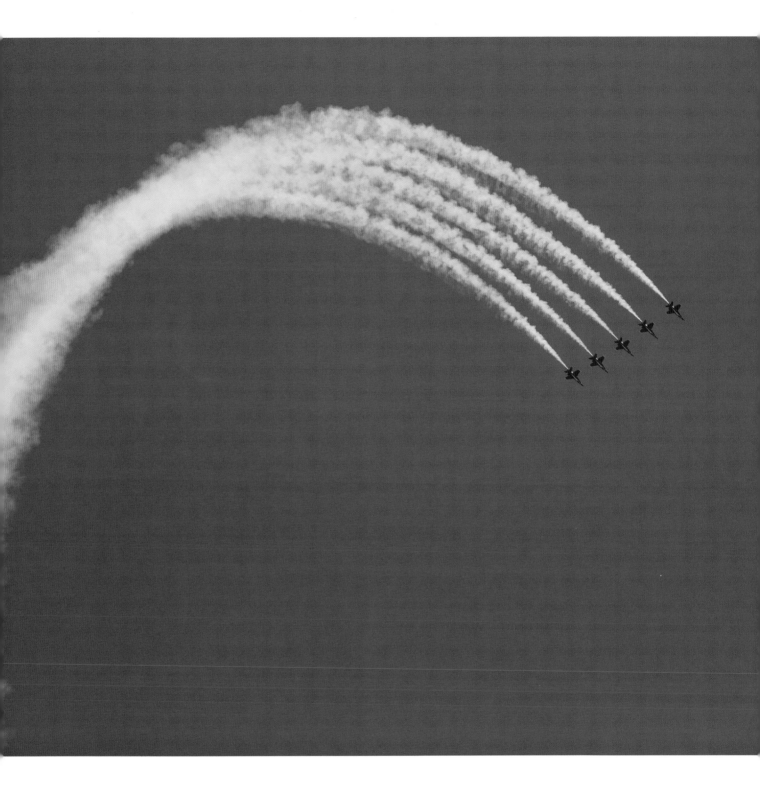

Smoke On

The U.S. Navy Blue Angels perform a
precise six-jet maneuver with "Smoke On"
during a break in the Seafair Hydroplane
Races. Long after their performance is
over, the jets leave a lingering cloud of
smoke over Lake Washington and the city.
Since 1946, the Blue Angels have performed for more than 463 million fans.

Seafair Parade of Ships

Navy personnel stand at attention on the USS *Bunker Hill* (CG-52) guided missile cruiser during Seafair's annual Parade of Ships across Elliott Bay. Overhead, a "Parade of Flight" showcases aviators in vintage and contemporary aircraft. Everyone enjoys the jubilant energy of Seafair Fleet Week and the Boeing Maritime Celebration.

Seafair Fleet Week

A special Navy tugboat from Bremerton joins the Seafair fun on Elliott Bay. The best place to watch the spectacular arrival of the Fleet is at Pier 62/63 along the Seattle Waterfront. During Seafair Fleet Week, the public has a unique opportunity to tour the ships and meet the sailors who operate them.

Seattle Fireboat Display

The Seattle Fire Department is ready for salt or freshwater action with its fleet of firefighting boats. The 108-foot *Leschi*, built in 2007, can fight marine fires with 22,000 gallons of water per minute and travel at 14 knots. When not showing off its spigot-power, the boat is stationed at Fire Station 5 on Elliott Bay.

Parade of Ships (top)

Seafair Fleet Week has been a Seattle tradition since 1950 when Navy ships such as the USS *Halsey* and USS *New Orleans* arrive to celebrate Seafair. During Seattle's premiere summertime festival, Fleet Week honors the men and women of the military who proudly and courageously serve our country.

Washington State Ferry (bottom)

One of the best ways to enjoy the beautiful scenery of the Emerald City is to hop a ferry to Bainbridge Island or Bremerton from downtown Seattle. Local residents use the ferries for birthday parties, anniversaries, and weddings. A walk-on ferry ride is an inexpensive way to take a scenic cruise across Elliott Bay and Puget Sound.

CenturyLink Field Event Center *(top)*

Seahawks fans dressed in green and blue pack CenturyLink Field during an NFL home game. The Seattle Sounders FC play their soccer matches here, as do high school and college football teams. With a 72,000-seat capacity and open-air views of downtown Seattle, the arena also hosts concerts, trade shows, and special events.

Ballard Locks *(bottom)*

The Hiram M. Chittenden Locks in Seattle's Ballard neighborhood have been moving boats from Puget Sound to and from the Ship Canal, Lake Union, and Lake Washington since 1917. Every year over a million tons of cargo pass through the locks, as do thousands of sockeye, coho, and Chinook salmon that leap up the 21-stage fish ladder.

Gas Works Park *(top)*

A seaplane takes off from Lake Union over the obsolete gas-processing plant that gave Gas Works Park its name. Used to convert coal to gas, the retired structures have been converted into picnic shelters, play areas, and a historic site. The 19-acre park is also accessible by bike on the popular Burke-Gilman Trail.

Seattle Urban Renewal *(bottom)*

Seattle has a long history of urban renewal from rebuilding after the Great Seattle Fire of 1889 to sluicing Denny Hill into Elliott Bay in the early 1900s. Gas Works Park is another prime example. It offers an unobstructed skyline view and is an enjoyable spot to watch Lake Union boating fun, like the sheet-snapping Duck Dodge sailboat races in summer.

Museum of History and Industry (top)

MOHAI is the largest private heritage organization in the State of Washington. Moved to the former Naval Reserve Building (Armory) on South Lake Union, and reopened in 2012, the stunning new museum features Seattle's history, educational programs, and new gallery space dedicated to large-scale touring exhibits.

Family Fourth at Lake Union (bottom)

Seattle is a party city and one of the biggest parties of the year takes place every Fourth of July. Crowds gather early at Gasworks Park in anticipation of the spectacular fireworks display over Lake Union synchronized to tunes like "Shake your Body." It's a joyful annual ritual not to be missed.

South Lake Union (opposite)

In addition to expensive yachts, wonderful shoreline restaurants and the 12-acre Lake Union Park, the recently refurbished South Lake Union area is also a biotech/biomedical hub that includes the Fred Hutchinson Cancer Research Center, Seattle Children's Hospital, University of Washington Medicine, and the Seattle Cancer Care Alliance.

Frye Art Museum *(top)*

Located on Seattle's First Hill, the Frye Art Museum opened its doors in 1952. It is the living legacy of Charles and Emma Frye, prominent early 20th-century Seattle business leaders and art collectors who amassed a notable collection of 19th- and 20th-century American, German, and French paintings.

Architectural Modernism *(bottom)*

American architect Paul Thiry is known as the father of architectural modernism in the Pacific Northwest. The Frye Art Museum is an excellent example of his work. The Frye displays a variety of paintings, prints, and sculptures. Internationally renowned and emerging artists are routinely showcased and admission is always free.

The Boeing Airplane Company *(top)*

Affectionately called the "Red Barn," this historic building once housed the original Boeing Company started by William E. Boeing in 1916. Boeing's transformation of the Pacific Northwest into a major aeronautical center is a source of great civic pride and the reason why Seattle is sometimes referred to as "Jet City."

Museum of Flight *(bottom)*

Aircraft appear to fly through the glass-walled Great Gallery at the Museum of Flight. Located at Boeing Field, the museum chronicles the history of aviation from da Vinci to the Space Age. In the foreground is a replica of the Boeing B & W, the first plane designed and built by Boeing and flown by Mr. Boeing himself in 1916.

Klondike Gold Rush National Historical Park - Seattle *(above)*

This fascinating Seattle-to-Alaska park is located in the historic Cadillac Hotel. It explains Seattle's critical role as the staging area for the Klondike Gold Rush. Gold fever hit in 1897 when the SS *Portland* arrived in Seattle carrying 68 miners with nearly two tons of gold. The rush was on!

Bellevue Arts Museum *(left)*

Emphasizing regional artists, the Bellevue Arts Museum is the Pacific Northwest's center for the exploration of art, craft, and design through thought-provoking exhibitions and programs. Every July, for nearly 70 years, the museum has hosted the revered BAM ARTSfair, the longest-running fair in downtown Bellevue.

Seattle Art Museum *(opposite)*

Artist Jonathan Borofsky created the 13-ton, 48-foot-tall *Hammering Man* sculpture in 1992. Affectionately known as "flatman," he is only seven inches thick. SAM exhibits artwork from across cultures, exploring the connections between past and present with over 23,000 pieces of art.

The Clog Factory (top)

Women with a shoe fetish will love this store. Located in Pioneer Square, the unique shop offers over 100 different styles of clogs from zebra-striped, plaid-clothed, and hand-painted to metallic gold. The healthy footwear is ideal for those who are on their feet all day, and the owner gives a discount to employees who do so.

Seattle Children's Museum (bottom)

Located in the Seattle Center Armory, this hands-on museum is designed for kids ages ten and younger. It offers 22,000-square feet of exploratory space, over a dozen exhibits, and a variety of stimulating programs. The museum encourages parents to engage with their kids through interactive play and learning.

EMP Museum (opposite)

Conceived by Microsoft co-founder Paul Allen and designed by architect Frank Gehry, the Experience Music Project Museum features this self-playing sculpture called *IF VI WAS IX: Roots and Branches*. Made with more than 500 instruments, the multi-story "guitar tornado" was designed by Neal Potter and built by Trimpin as a tribute to American music.

Fremont Summer Solstice Parade

Begun in 1972, the Fremont Fair each June draws thousands of people to Seattle's offbeat Fremont neighborhood. The biggest attraction is the colorfully outlandish Solstice Parade celebrating the start of summer. Participants don outfits that are visually stunning, sometimes achieved with nothing more than body paint.

Market Theater Gum Wall

Designated a Seattle tourist attraction since 1999, the giant gooey, dripping gum wall is located in Post Alley under the Pike Place Market. Covered with used chewing gum in delectable colors, some shaped into small artworks, the gum wall was named the second "germiest" tourist attraction in the world by CNN in 2009.

Crab Pot Seafood Restaurant *(opposite, top)*

Pick up a wooden hammer, put on a plastic bib, and get ready to whack some crab at this famous waterfront restaurant. Located at Miners Landing on Pier 57, the Crab Pot specializes in "Seafeast" meals that include an assortment of cooked seafood that is literally dumped right onto your paper tablecloth.

Rachel the Pig *(opposite, bottom)*

The beloved mascot of Pike Place Market is probably the most photographed and love-polished brass pig on the planet. Created in 1986 by Washington artist Georgia Gerber, this 550-pound piggy bank has raised over $200,000 to help low income and elderly residents of downtown Seattle.

Pike Place Market *(above)*

Founded in 1907, Pike Place Market is the oldest continuously operating farmers' market in the United States. Overlooking Elliott Bay, Seattle's historic market offers delicious things to munch, collectible artwork, entertaining street musicians, and the best people watching in town.

Flower Vendors

During spring and summer, an explosion of fresh flowers line the walls of Pike Place Market. Here it is possible to buy a large bouquet for only five dollars. Wedding planners frequently take advantage of the affordable prices for fresh floral arrangements available in creative styles and colors.

Market Grill Sign *(above)*

This humorous electrified salmon enhances the visual fun of exploring the Pike Place Market. In addition to advertising our region's love affair with everything salmon, the colorful fish is pointing to the Market Grill Restaurant best known for their award-winning chowder and grilled salmon sandwiches.

Seattle Seafood *(right)*

Begun in 1911, the Pure Food Fish Market at Pike Place Market has been family owned and operated for four generations. Here, great-grandson Isaac Behar holds a fresh-caught 30- to 35-pound king salmon. From clams, oysters, and giant scallops to lobster tails and king crab legs, all of their seafood can be packed and shipped anywhere in the United States.

Starbucks Birthplace *(opposite)*

Street musicians called the Tallboys perform foot-stomping, old-time fiddling in front of the original Starbucks store that first opened in 1971 at Pike Place Market. The historically preserved store still looks very much like it did then. Today, Starbucks specialty coffees are sold in more than 17,000 retail stores in over 55 countries.

JP Patches Statue *(above, left)*

From 1958 to 1981, Julius Pierpont Patches, (portrayed by Chris Wedes), hosted the longest-running children's TV show in American history. This beloved clown lived in the city dump and wore a rumpled hat and a patchwork coat. Now he and Gertrude dance on forever as a bronze statue in Fremont's Solstice Plaza.

Jimmy Hendrix Statue *(above, right)*

Kneeling at the corner of Broadway and Pine on Capitol Hill, Jimi Hendrix continues to wail on his electric guitar. Created by Northwest artist Daryl Smith and unveiled in a "purple haze" in 1997, the bronze sculpture honors our legendary Seattle native who gifted the world with the Jimi Hendrix Experience.

Carousel at Pier 57 *(above)*

Painted "flying horses" spin to lively circus music as delighted children big and small ride the historic Pier 57 Carousel. The vintage 20th-century merry-go-round is located at Miner's Landing on the Seattle Waterfront. The adjacent Seattle Waterfront Arcade, loaded with games, promises the biggest selection of prizes in the Northwest.

Teatro ZinZanni *(left)*

Described as "the Kit Kat Klub on acid" and "the hottest ticket in town," Teatro ZinZanni is crazy good fun. Buckle your seat belt for a magical, three-hour whirlwind of international cirque, comedy, and cabaret artists all served up with a five-course feast. But be forewarned: You just might become part of the show.

Bill Spiedel's Underground Tour (above)

Don't miss this hilarious historic tour into the bowels of Seattle. Entertaining guides share the dirt, corruption, and scandalous stories of fledgling Seattle as they lead you through dark subterranean storefronts on abandoned sidewalks entombed after the Great Fire of 1889. The tour starts at Doc Maynard's, a restored 1890s saloon.

Underground Seattle (right)

An old Samis sign hints at the long real estate history behind the present-day Samis Foundation based in Pioneer Square. Above, a skylight with purple-hued panes of glass lets in light from the sidewalk above at First and Yesler. The skylight's prisms are opaque enough to recognize pedestrians without seeing any details.

Purple Café and Wine Bar (top)

Their floor-to-ceiling "wine tower" has over 600 bottle selections making it possible to pair fine global wines with classic American cuisine prepared with the freshest Northwest ingredients. Purple's wine program won the "Award of Ultimate Distinction" from *Wine Enthusiast* magazine and was named "Best Wine Bar" by *Evening Magazine*.

REI (bottom)

Lloyd and Mary Anderson founded Recreational Equipment International in 1938. Famed mountaineer Jim Whittaker was REI's first employee. Today, the sporting goods company has millions of members and generates nearly $2 billion annually. The 65-foot-tall Climbing Pinnacle lit up at night, showcases REI's 1996 Flagship store.

New Year's Eve Celebration (opposite)

New Year's Eve fireworks explode over the Space Needle. Synchronized to music, the spectacular, computer-controlled pyrotechnic display is triggered from the roof of the Needle at midnight. Meanwhile, partygoers in the revolving SkyCity Restaurant continue to spin, thanks to a motor with the highest gear ratio in the world: 360,000 to 1.

5th Avenue Theatre (top)

This historic theatre with a beautiful, Chinese-inspired interior opened in 1926 as a venue for vaudeville and film. Since then, it has become an incubator for 14 new musicals, five which moved on to Broadway to earn a combined 14 Tony Awards, including two for Best Musical (*Hairspray* and *Memphis*).

Benaroya Hall (bottom)

The acoustically superb Benaroya Hall is home to the award-winning Seattle Symphony. The 2,500-seat hall presents the popular Live @ Benaroya Hall Series. It is also a popular venue for business meetings and local performing arts groups, such as the 300-member Seattle Men's Chorus, the largest community chorus in the U.S.

Paramount Theatre (opposite)

Managed by the Seattle Theatre Group, this famous theatre was built by Hollywood's Paramount Pictures and opened in 1928. They transformed a ravine with a creek into a glamorous Versailles-styled movie palace with a French Renaissance interior. The theatre has been hosting "Shows Divine at 9th and Pine" ever since.

Lake View Cemetery *(top)*

Located on Capitol Hill, this historic cemetery is often referred to as the "pioneer cemetery" since most of Seattle's founding fathers are buried here. Princess Angeline, the eldest daughter of Chief Seattle was buried here in 1896. Her restless ghost is sometimes seen walking through Pike Place Market or riding the ferry to Bainbridge.

Bruce Lee Gravesite *(bottom)*

Lake View Cemetery is the final resting place of renowned Chinese martial artist Bruce Lee, and his son Brandon. They are the most frequently visited graves in the cemetery. Admirers leave behind flowers, pebbles, and other sentimental treasures to show their affection for this pop culture, Kung Fu icon of the 20th century.

"... AND SO IT'S GOODNIGHT

MY DARLING,

I SEND YOU ALL MY LOVE."

LETTER TO A SWEETHEART

Benaroya Hall Garden of Remembrance

This half-acre garden quietly memorializes more than 8,000 Washington State veterans who died since 1941. On Memorial Day, residents gather here to honor the fallen heroes. The little urban oasis has slender reflecting pools, water cascades, and trees and flower beds. The names engraved in granite are warmed by the afternoon sun.

107

Seattle Fallen Firefighters Memorial *(above)*

The dramatic sculpture of bronze and granite was designed by Hai Ying Wu in 1998. Inspired by the four firefighters who died while fighting a warehouse fire in Seattle's International District in 1995, the *Fallen Firefighter's Memorial* in Occidental Park is a tribute to all Washington State firefighters who have died in the line of duty.

Coast Guard Museum *(opposite, top)*

This hidden treasure is tucked away on Pier 36 along the Seattle Waterfront. On display are ship steering wheels, Coast Guard uniforms, a piece of the HMS *Bounty*, the Coast Guard flag carried aboard the first Space Shuttle flight, and part of "Old Ironsides," the USS *Constitution*. Admission to this fascinating place is always free.

Seattle Metropolitan Police Museum
(opposite, bottom)

The Pioneer Square Historic District is home to The Seattle Metropolitan Police Museum. Working in collaboration with the Seattle Police Department and the King County Sheriff's Office, the museum offers insight into transitions experienced by both agencies since the early 1860s.

Green Lake Park (top)

One of Seattle's most beloved parks, Green Lake Park attracts thousands of people each day. The 2.8-mile path around the lake provides the perfect recreational outlet for runners, bikers, skaters, and walkers. It's a great place to exercise, people watch, and enjoy the endless entertainment of dogs on parade.

Danny Woo Garden (bottom)

The Danny Woo International District Community Garden is a special park in the heart of downtown Seattle. Encompassing 1.5 acres, it is the largest green space in the Chinatown-International District. This lovely park features picnic benches, public art, walking trails, and more than 100 spaces for community gardening.

Lenin Statue (opposite)

A young boy is dwarfed by the 16-foot-tall bronze statue of Lenin in the heart of the Fremont neighborhood. Created in the 1970s by Slavic artist Emil Venkov, the statue stood in Poprad, Czechoslovakia before being toppled during the revolution of 1989. Today, the 30-ton sculpture is a reminder that art can outlive politics.

University of Washington

Founded in 1861 with a private gift of 10 acres in what is now the heart of downtown Seattle, UW is one of the oldest public universities on the West Coast. It is also one of the most beautiful. Located on the shores of Union and Portage bays, it enrolls more than 50,000 students a year.

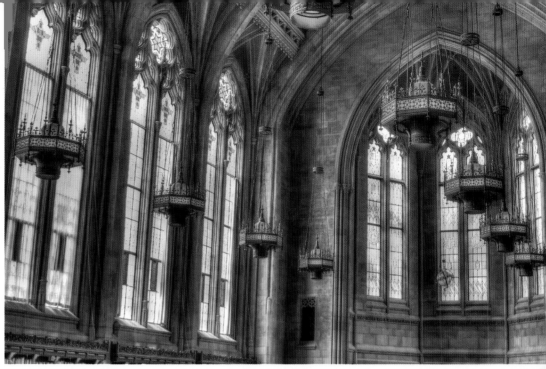

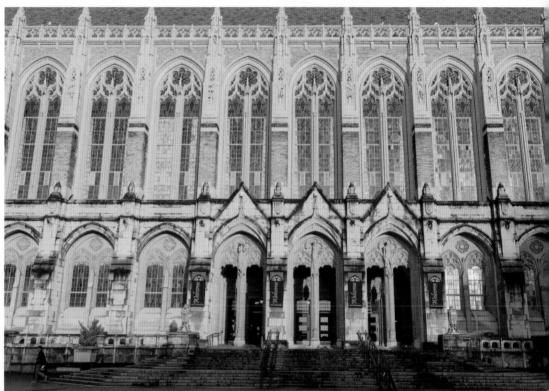

Suzzallo Library Reading Room *(top)*

Past University of Washington President, Henry Suzzallo, believed that universities should be "cathedrals of learning." The Suzzallo Reading Room reflects this idea with cathedral-like arches, tall stained-glass windows, ornate lighting, and a 65-foot-high timber-vaulted ceiling. Suzzallo considered the library "the soul of the university."

Suzzallo Library Exterior *(bottom)*

Echoing the great halls of Oxford and Cambridge colleges, the University of Washington's Suzzallo Library opened in 1927. This Gothic "Cathedral of books" is only part of the university's extensive library system. In 2011 the Sierra Club honored the university for being the most environmentally minded college in the U.S.

Henry Art Gallery

Contemporary art collections and special exhibitions at "the Henry" stimulate research and teaching at the University of Washington and provide a creative wellspring for artists, students, and educators alike. The gallery explores trends from the advent of photography in the mid-19th century to the modern art and design of today.

Flowering Cherry Trees *(opposite, top)*

Thousands of people flock to the University of Washington "Quad" every spring to witness the annual blooming of the Yoshino cherry trees. It is a sight not to be missed. As the floral event peaks then wanes, the ground is literally covered with pink "snow." This unique horticultural tradition has long roots back to 1964.

Burke Museum *(opposite, bottom)*

Native American carvings greet visitors at the entrance to the much-cherished Burke Museum located on the University of Washington campus. The museum safeguards our region's cultural heritage and extensive Washington State natural history collections, sharing the knowledge that makes them meaningful.

Northwest Coffee Culture *(above)*

The Vashon Island Coffee Roasterie creates their fine gourmet coffees using rare beans that are high-mountain, shade-grown, and traditionally farmed. Housed in a century-old building, the Roasterie features a coffee museum, local art, good music, and friendly locals willing to share tall tales over a cup of brew.

GIRAFFE *(opposite)*

Located on Vashon Island, GIRAFFE specializes in beautiful hand-crafted artwork from around the world. Weaving together beauty and justice, owner Priscilla Schleigh has established an international circle of fair trade that benefits artisans in developing countries. She estimates over 10,000 hands have created her collectible treasures.

Indian Salmon Bake *(above, left)*

For centuries, Native Americans in the Pacific Northwest have cooked salmon on a wood frame before an open fire. Attached to a split branch of cedar or ironwood, the boned fish is leaned toward the fire and slow roasted. The tradition continues at Tillicum Village, where they have been cooking salmon this way for over 50 years.

Tillicum Village Dancer *(above, right)*

Music and dance are important traditions of the Coast Salish people, as is storytelling. Stories were passed down through families with lessons about behavior, family connections, and relationships with the spirit world. Here a costumed Native American dancer interprets a traditional story at Tillicum Village on Blake Island.

Blake Island (above)

After a narrated Argosy Cruise to Blake Island, guests arrive at Tillicum Village for a traditional salmon bake. There are many beautiful examples of native artwork here, including several hand-carved cedar totem poles. This vertical art form originated among the Haida, Tlingit, and Tshimshian people from Alaska and British Columbia.

Bald Eagle (right)

The bald eagle is one of the largest birds of prey with a wingspan of over six feet. Once threatened with extinction, they now thrive in abundance throughout the Pacific Northwest. Bald eagles are sacred to Native American people. They believe these high-flying "masters of the sky" symbolize truth, freedom, strength and honor, and represent the divine spirit.

Daybreak Star Indian Cultural Center

A young participant waits to perform during the Seafair Pow Wow at Discovery Park. The goal of the United Indians of All Tribes Foundation (UIATF), based at Daybreak Star, is to empower and preserve a strong sense of tribal identity, culture, tradition, and wellbeing for all indigenous people in and around Puget Sound.

A Proud Heritage

Indigenous people of the Americas dream of one day awakening to a new century of light, a period of renewal. As they rediscover their own strengths and greatness bestowed upon them by the Creator, they will impact the world. Founded in 1970, the United Indians of All Tribes Foundation serves as a focal point for this renewal.

Nordic Heritage Museum *(above)*

Located in Ballard, this is the only museum in the United States to honor the legacy of immigrants from the five Nordic countries: Denmark, Finland, Iceland, Norway, and Sweden. The Scandinavian Studies program at the University of Washington, established in 1909, is the largest program of its kind outside of Scandinavia.

Seattle Asian Art Museum *(opposite)*

This wonderful art deco building in Volunteer Park reopened in 1994 as the Seattle Asian Art Museum. It is a showcase for the Seattle Art Museum's world-renowned Asian collections and a community hub for Asian culture. The museum features the magnificent art of China, Korea, Japan, India, the Himalayas, and Southeast Asia.

COLORS OF THE OASIS
CENTRAL ASIAN IKATS

MARCH 15-AUGUST 5

Historic Chinatown Gate (above)

Generous contributions to the Historic Chinatown Gate Foundation made it possible for Seattle's Chinese community to realize their dream to build a traditional Chinese gate, or *pai-lau*, to commemorate their presence in Seattle's Chinatown-International District. Built with steel, pressure-treated wood, and ceramic materials, the symbolic gate reflects ancient Chinese palace architecture.

Dragon Pole (left)

A fierce red dragon climbs a light pole in Seattle's Chinatown-International District. The fiberglass creature is one of many attractions in this historic part of Seattle. Try a dim sum lunch, bubble tea made with chewy black tapioca balls, or a hot bowl of Phở in any one of 85 restaurants here. In July, McDonald's sponsors the Dragon Festival with over 30 cultural performances that include Japanese *taiko* drumming, martial arts demos, and spirited Chinese lion and dragon dances.

Northwest African American Museum
(above)

What does it mean to be African American in the Pacific Northwest? According to NAAM, it is a beautiful range of colors and hues, with a rich diversity of people, cultures, and life experiences. Opened in 2008, the Northwest African American Museum invites you to explore this continually evolving story.

Northwest African American Museum Exhibits *(right)*

The primary goal of NAAM is to share the history, arts, and cultures of all people of African descent. The best way to accomplish this is by exploring and celebrating Black experiences in America through exhibitions, educational programs, and special events.

Ten Feet into the Future *(above)*

Five metal figures sprint from a stand of birch trees toward the setting sun. Created by David Govedare in 1986, this contemporary sculpture can be seen along the north side of the Olympic Sculpture Park. A gifted artist, Govedare is able to make rigid, hard metal appear supple, full of movement, and very much alive.

Chief Seattle Fountain and Pergola *(bottom)*

The Chief Seattle fountain was designed by James Wehn. Nearby, the famous glass and cast iron Pergola was once used as a cable car stop. Both were created for the Alaska-Yukon-Pacific Exposition in 1909. The Pioneer Square Historic District protects the largest collection of Victorian and Romanesque architecture in the country.

Chief Seattle *(opposite)*

Seattle was named for Chief (Sealth) Seattle, the powerful Chief of the Duwamish and Suquamish people. This copper statue, also by James Wehn, was unveiled by the Chief's great-great-granddaughter, Myrtle Loughery, on Founders Day in 1912. A loyal friend to the first white settlers, Chief Seattle gestures a permanent greeting at Tilikum Place.

As one of Seattle's leading stock and assignment photographers, Stuart Westmorland specializes in cityscapes, lifestyle, and marine photography. His images have been published on more than 200 magazine covers including *Time, Outside, National Wildlife* and *Ritz Carlton* and used for many book covers including Bill Bryson's *In a Sunburned Country* and Wilbur Smith's *The Triumph of the Sun.*

Stuart won the top honor at the 2010 International Conservation Photography Awards. Founded by Art Wolfe, the award is given to the photographer whose image best exemplifies the mission of the ICP Awards—"the advancement of photography as a unique medium capable of bringing awareness and preservation to our environment through art."

A fulltime photographer since 1992, Stuart has traveled the world on assignment for many magazines including *Skin Diver* and *Ocean Sports International.* He was a contributing regional editor for *Pacific Diver, Australasia Scuba Diver, Aqua, Sport Diver, Scuba Diving* and *Asian Geographic.* Corporate assignments include: trade ads and brochure images for Talus Corporation; travel images from South America for Holland America; feature photography for Lexus Magazine in Japan to cover the Cherry Blossom Festival and trade ads for American Express, the National Geographic Society, American Online, Eddie Bauer, The Gap, MCI and Microsoft, to name just a few.

Currently Stuart, his wife Robin and stepson Oliver reside in Mill Creek, Washington.

Images in this book are available for use in publication as well as décor prints for home or office by contacting: www.stuartwestmorland.com.

Barbara Sleeper is a freelance science and travel writer. Her articles have appeared in numerous national and international publications including *Audubon, Australian Natural History, Pacific Discovery, Anima, Das Tier, Life, Wildlife Art News, Travel & Leisure, Travel Holiday, Ranger Rick, Sport Diver* and *Ocean Geographic.* She also worked as a contributing editor for both *Animals* and *AirCal* magazines. Ms. Sleeper has written several books including *Ocean Duets* (2006), *Vanishing Act* (2005), *Our Seattle* (2002), *In the Company of Manatees* (2000), *Seattle: A CityLife Pictorial Guide* (1998), *Primates: The Amazing World of Lemurs, Monkeys and Apes* (1997), *Alligators: Beneath the Blackwater* (1996), *Wild Cats of the World* (1995) and *Migrations: Wildlife in Motion* (1994). Barbara lives in Bothell, Washington and can be contacted for assignments at www.barbsleeper.com.